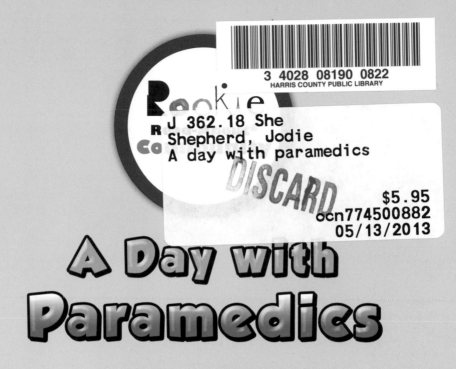

A Day with Paramedics

by Jodie Shepherd

Content Consultant
Jerry Bedingfield, EMT

Reading Consultant
Jeanne Clidas, Ph.D.
Reading Specialist

Children's Press®
An Imprint of Scholastic Inc
New York Toronto London Auckland
Mexico City New Delhi Hong K
Danbury, Connecticut

Library of Congress Cataloging-in-Publication Data
Shepherd, Jodie.
  A day with paramedics / by Jodie Shepherd.
     p. cm. — (Rookie read-about community)
  Includes index.
  ISBN 978-0-531-28954-9 (library binding) — ISBN 978-0-531-29254-9 (pbk.)
  1. Emergency medical technicians—Juvenile literature. 2. Emergency medical
services—Juvenile literature. I. Title.
RA645.5.S56 2013
362.18—dc23   2012013358

Produced by Spooky Cheetah Press

1 2 3 4 5 6 7 8 9 10 R 22 21 20 19 18 17 16 15 14 13

Photographs © 2013: Alamy Images/Spencer Grant: 8; iStockphoto: 19 (Margo
Harrison), 15 (Nancy Louie); PhotoEdit/Tom Carter: 23; Shutterstock, Inc./
Rechitan Sorin: 28; Thinkstock: 7, 11 (Getty Images), cover, 3 top, 16, 31 top right
(iStockphoto), 12 (Keith Brofsky), 4, 31 bottom left (Photodisc), 3 bottom, 31 bottom
right (PhotoObjects.net), 20 (Ryan McVay), 24, 27, 31 top left.

Table of Contents

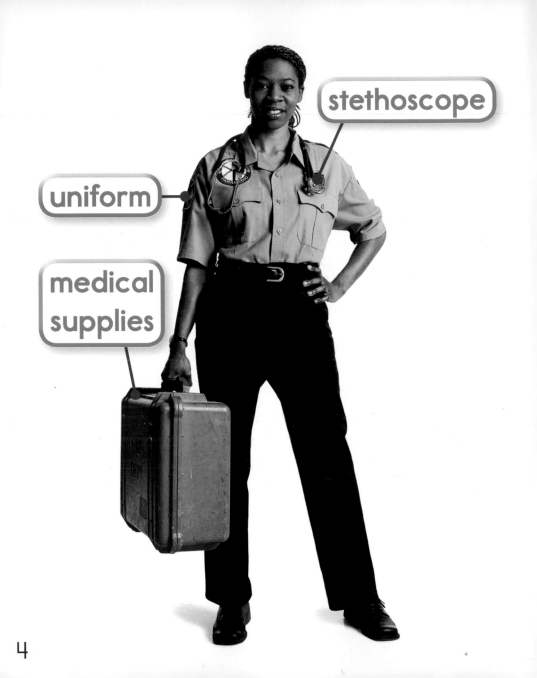

stethoscope

uniform

medical
supplies

Meet a Paramedic

There is an emergency!
Someone has dialed 911.
Paramedics are on the job.

Paramedics save lives. They take care of people who are hurt or sick. They get them to the hospital fast.

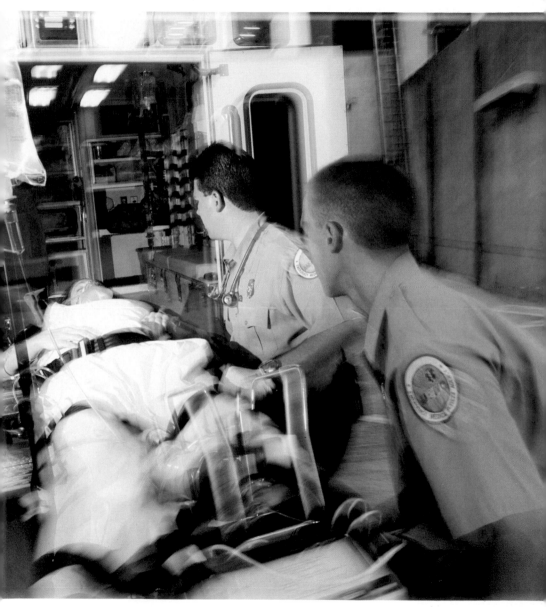

Here to Help!

You may see paramedics at football games, races, and fairs. Any time there are crowds of people, paramedics are there, ready for action.

When there is an accident, paramedics might work with police. Sometimes they work with firefighters.

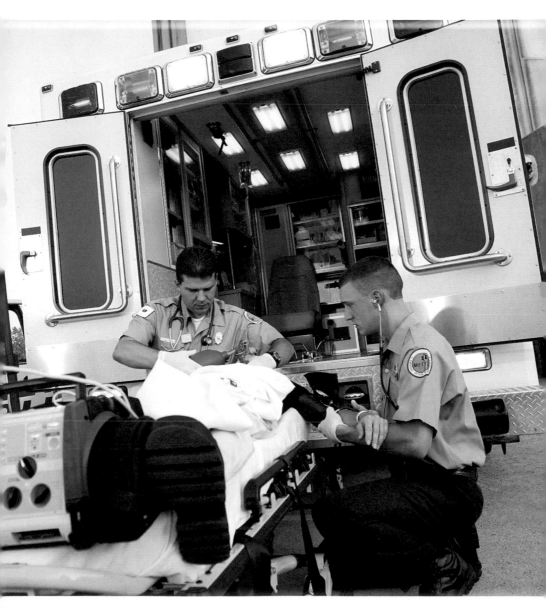

At the Scene

Paramedics know what to do in any emergency. They work quickly and calmly.

The paramedic's first job is to find out what is wrong. He checks the patient's heart. He may need to get the heart beating again.

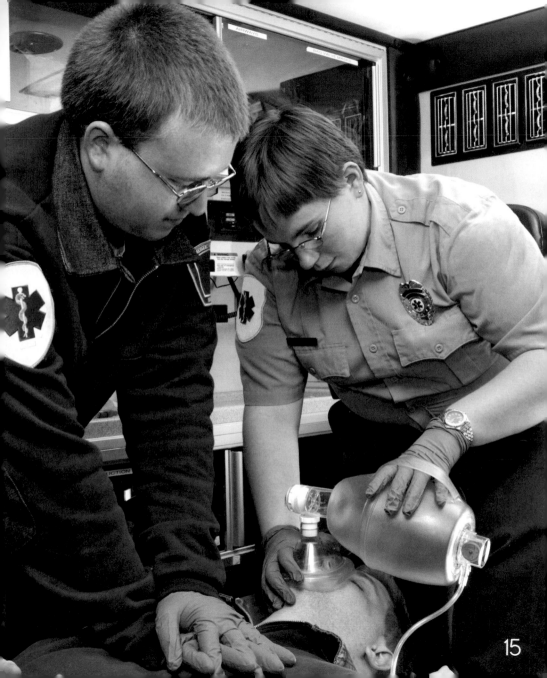

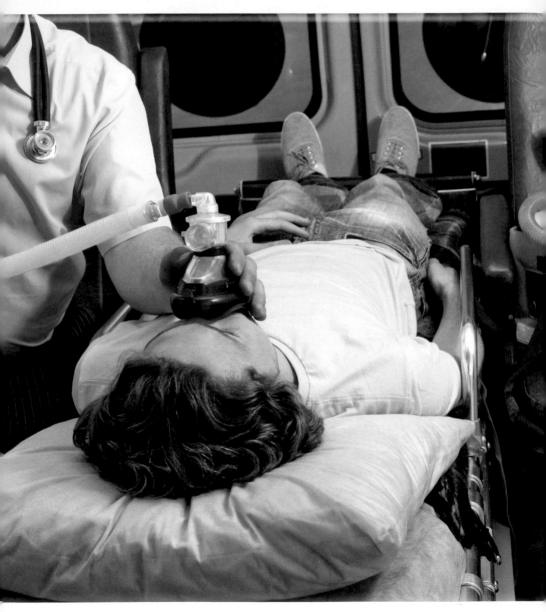

The paramedic may need to help the patient breathe.

When the patient is ready to travel, it is time to get to the hospital. The patient is moved to the ambulance on a backboard or stretcher.

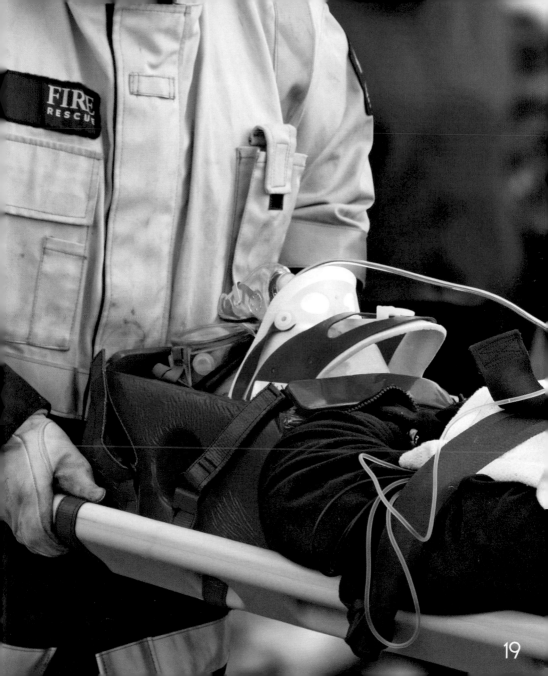

20

In the Ambulance

An ambulance is like an emergency room on wheels. It has everything the patient needs for now.

The paramedic rides with the patient to the hospital.

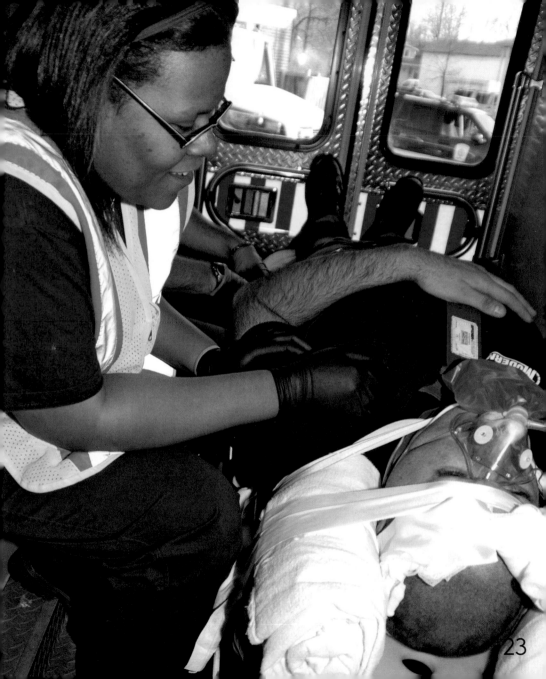

The ambulance arrives at the hospital. The paramedic gives the doctor a full report.

Always Ready

If you need help, a paramedic can get to you no matter where you are. In the mountains, paramedics may travel on skis or by snowmobile.

Paramedics may fly in by helicopter if a person is very hard to reach. Anywhere you are, paramedics are ready to help!

Try It! Look back at page 5. Pretend to dial 911. (Do not really call—only use 911 in a true emergency.) Pretend to tell the operator your name and address, and explain the emergency.

Be a Community Helper!

- When you are prepared, you are safe! Wear a helmet when you bike or skate.

- Wear your seat belt in a car.

- Swim only in safe areas. Make sure a grown-up is watching. Use sunscreen.

- Know how to call 911 for help.

- Only call 911 in a true emergency.

Words You Know

ambulance

helicopter

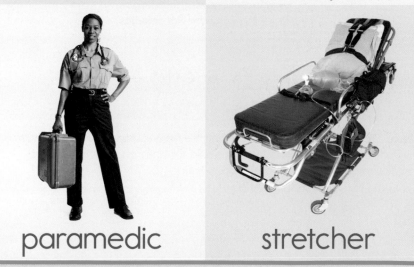

paramedic

stretcher

Index

Facts for Now

Visit this Scholastic Web site for more information on paramedics:
www.factsfornow.scholastic.com
Enter the keyword **Paramedics**

About the Author

Jodie Shepherd, who also writes under the name Leslie Kimmelman, is an award-winning author of dozens of books for children, both fiction and nonfiction. She is also a children's book editor.